KQPIANOS / YUAN KEVIN QIU

COMPOSER OF THE 5 PIECES

All composed through his spark of ideas, these 5 pieces will surely make piano playing fun.

@KQPIANOS ON SPOTIFY

For all 5 pieces, my fingering is only a suggestion. Use your own fingering if you find it comfortable

RIVER

This piece was composed when I was hiking in a local trail. It is meant to depict a beautiful river flowing through such beautiful scenery.

IN THIS MOMENT

This piece was composed in 2021, where I wanted to show the hope of things getting better, thus we unite and win as human beings.

enjoy!

For all 5 pieces, my fingering is only a suggestion. Use your own fingering if you find it comfortable

MORNING

This piece was composed to depict the beautiful scenes of a sunny morning, with the sun rising and birds chirping., sometimes with cars zooming by.

SOUND OF SPRING

This piece was composed again when I was hiking, during a spring day. It is meant to symbolize the reborn of everything (plants, and so on).

enjoy!

For all 5 pieces, my fingering is only a suggestion. Use your own fingering if you find it comfortable

YEARS AGO

This piece was a special composition, where I wanted to depict my journey of learning the piano to majoring in music to composing and writing these pieces. This was inspired by Kevin Kern's Through Your Eyes.

Music Terms Sheet

rit.
gradually slow down

dim.
gradually get softer

Andante
Slow walking pace

Adagio
At a slow tempo

Fermata 
Hoooooold

Rolled Chords
Play chord arpeggiated from left to right quickly

8va

Play octave higher (8 notes)

Triplets, play 3 notes in the time of 2 notes

River

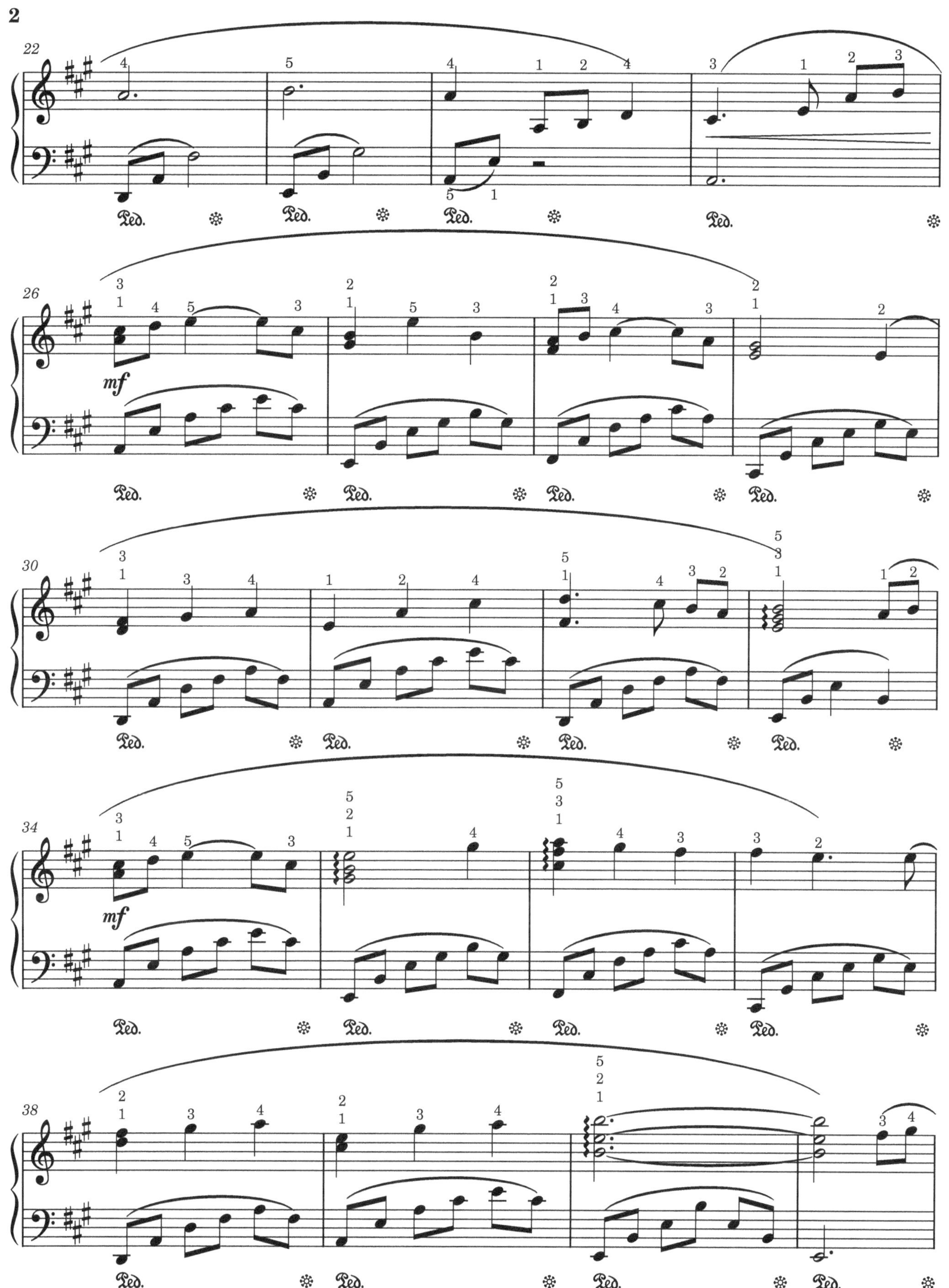

see fingering on previous pages for similar sections

mp
mf
Ped.
Ped.
Ped.
Ped.

103
hold for looooooong
107
5   2   3 2 1   2   1   2   3
111
mp
1
5
115
2 1   2
119
mf

123
dim.
Ped.
Ped.
Ped.
Ped.

127
p rit.
Ped.
Ped.
Ped.

In This Moment

Yuan (Kevin) Qiu

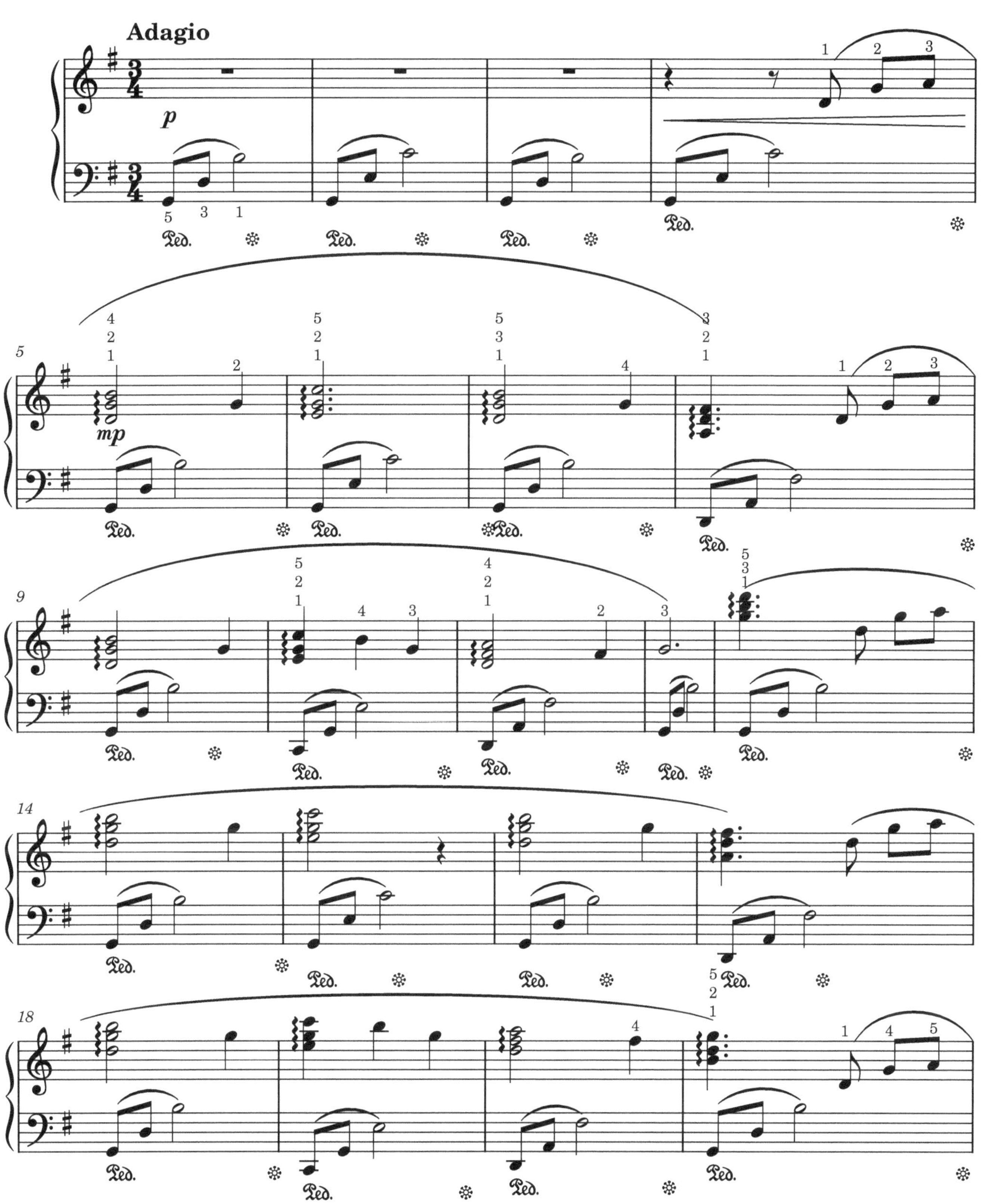

22
26
5 all across this section
30
mf
34
38

42
see previous pages for fingering
46
mp
Ped.
50
54
58
Ped.

62
mf
64
Ped.
68
Ped.
72
Ped.
76
Ped.
mp

97
rit.
5
4
pp
ppp
1
5
1
5
Ped.
Ped.
Ped.
Ped.

Morning

36
rit.
8
Ped.
40
mp
8
Ped.
44
8
8
Ped.
48
8
8
3
Ped.
52
8
8
Ped.

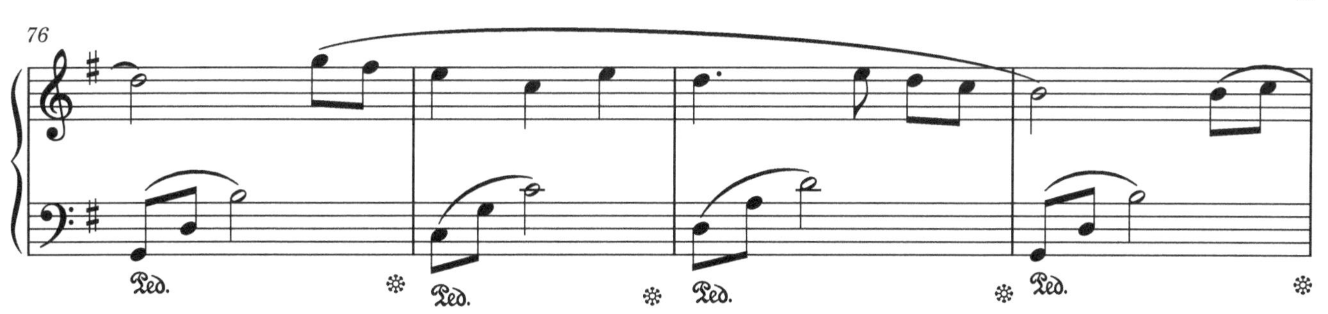

Sound of Spring

21
Yes, there's no R.H here, I didn't forget
use same fingering for similar sections
Ped.
Ped.
Ped.
Ped.
25
Ped.
Ped.
Ped.
Ped.
29
8
p
8
Ped.
Ped.
Ped.
Ped.
33
8
8
Ped.
Ped.
Ped.
Ped.
37
8
4
1
2
3 4
5
1
4
3
2
5
4
Ped.
Ped.
Ped.
Ped.

watch for tempo change
Adagio
mp
Andante
p
dim.
gradually get very slow
(dim.)
rit.
mp

Years Ago

17
21
mf
25
29
mf
33
Ped.
Ped.

use same fingering as previous key

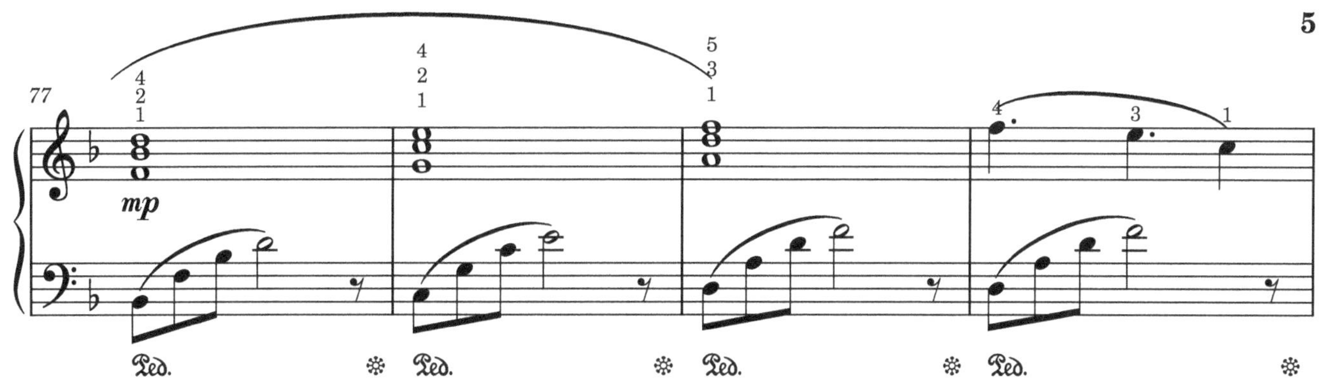
77
mp
Ped.
Ped.
Ped.
Ped.

81
rit.
p
Ped.
Ped.
Ped.
Ped.

Hope you had fun with the 5 pieces

www.ingramcontent.com/pod-product-compliance
Lightning Source LLC
Chambersburg PA
CBHW041043120726
48006CB00017B/2323